Numbers

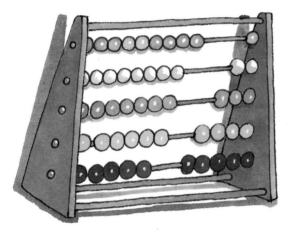

Los números

lohs *noo*-meh-rohs

Illustrated by Clare Beaton

Ilustraciones de Clare Beaton

BARRON'S

one

1 2 3 4 5 6 7 8 9 10

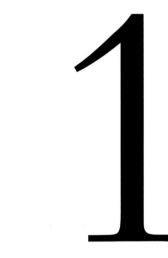

uno, una

oo-noh, *oo*-nah

two

1 2 3 4 5 6 7 8 9 10

1 2 3 4 5 6 7 8 9 10

2

dos

dohs

three

1 2 **3** 4 5 6 7 8 9 10

1 2 3 4 5 6 7 8 9 10

tres

trehs

four

1 2 3 4 5 6 7 8 9 10

1 2 3 4 5 6 7 8 9 10

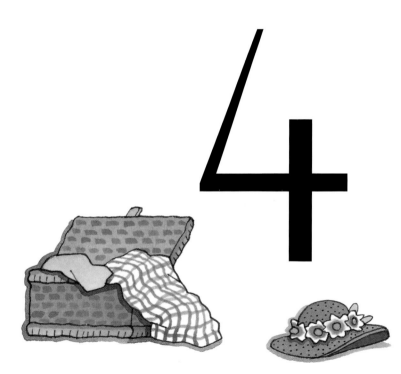

4

cuatro

kwah-troh

five

1 2 3 4 5 6 7 8 9 10

1 2 3 4 (5) 6 7 8 9 10

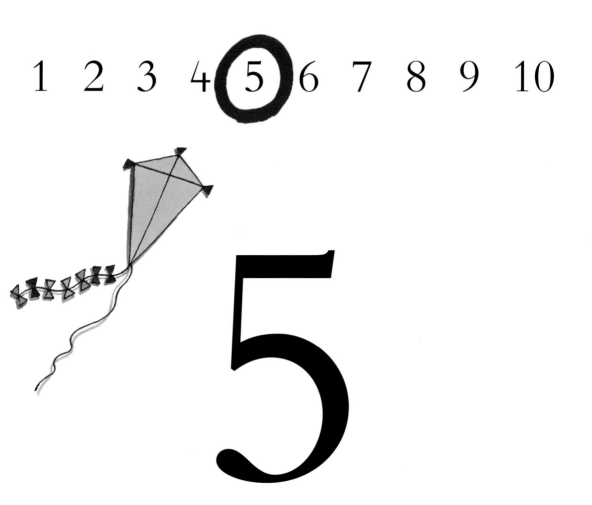

5

cinco

seen-koh

six

1 2 3 4 5 6 7 8 9 10

1 2 3 4 5 6 7 8 9 10

6

seis

seh–ees

seven

1 2 3 4 5 6 7 8 9 10

1 2 3 4 5 6 **7** 8 9 10

7

siete

see-*eh*-teh

eight

1 2 3 4 5 6 7 8 9 10

1 2 3 4 5 6 7 8 9 10

ocho

oh-choh

nine

1 2 3 4 5 6 7 8 9 10

nueve

noo-*eh*-veh

ten

1 2 3 4 5 6 7 8 9 10

10

diez

dee-ehs

1 2 3 4 5

one   two   three   four   five

uno,   dos   tres   cuatro   cinco
una

6 7 8 9 10

six	seven	eight	nine	ten
seis	siete	ocho	nueve	diez

A simple guide to pronouncing Spanish words

- Read this guide as naturally as possible, as if it were English.
- Put stress on the letters in *italics*, for example, *noo* in *noo*-meh-rohs.

Los números	lohs *noo*-meh-rohs	**Numbers**
uno, una	*oo*-noh, *oo*-nah	**one**
dos	dohs	**two**
tres	trehs	**three**
cuatro	*kwah*-troh	**four**
cinco	*seen*-koh	**five**
seis	*seh*-ees	**six**
siete	see-*eh*-teh	**seven**
ocho	*oh*-choh	**eight**
nueve	noo-*eh*-veh	**nine**
diez	dee-*ehs*	**ten**